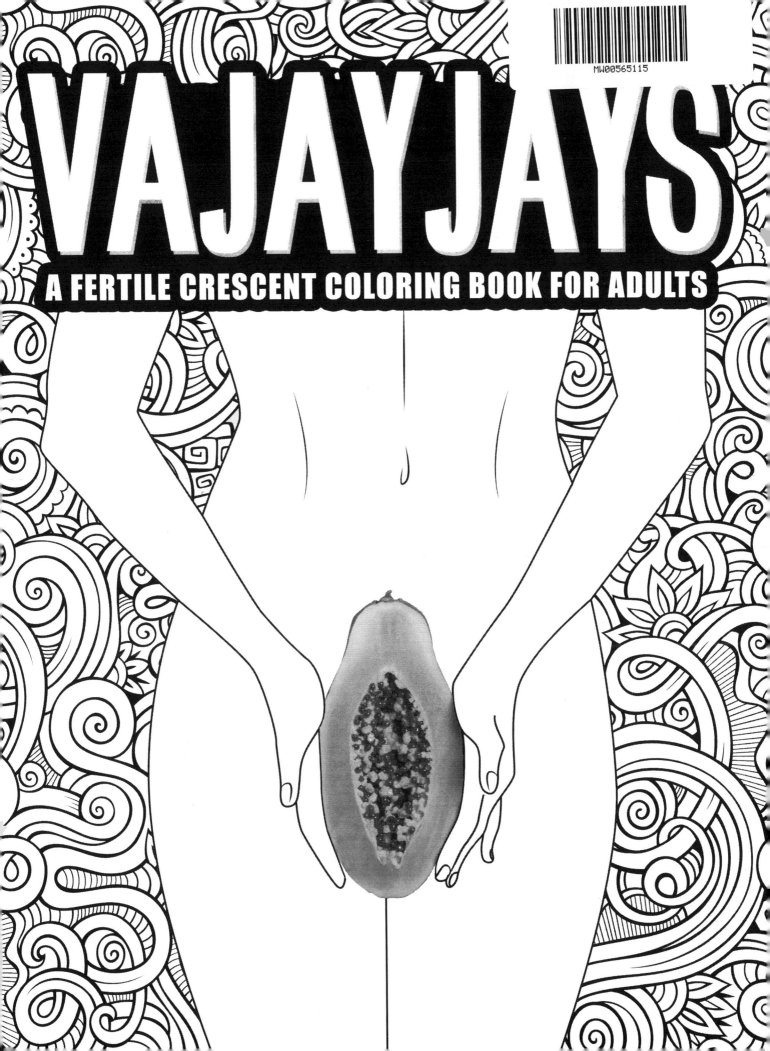

VAJAYJAYS

A FERTILE CRESCENT COLORING BOOK FOR ADULTS

FREE DOWNLOAD!

WHAT the FORK?!

AH, Shirt.

SON OF A BENCH!

YOUR CODE: VAG363

www.honeybadgercoloring.com/vajayjay

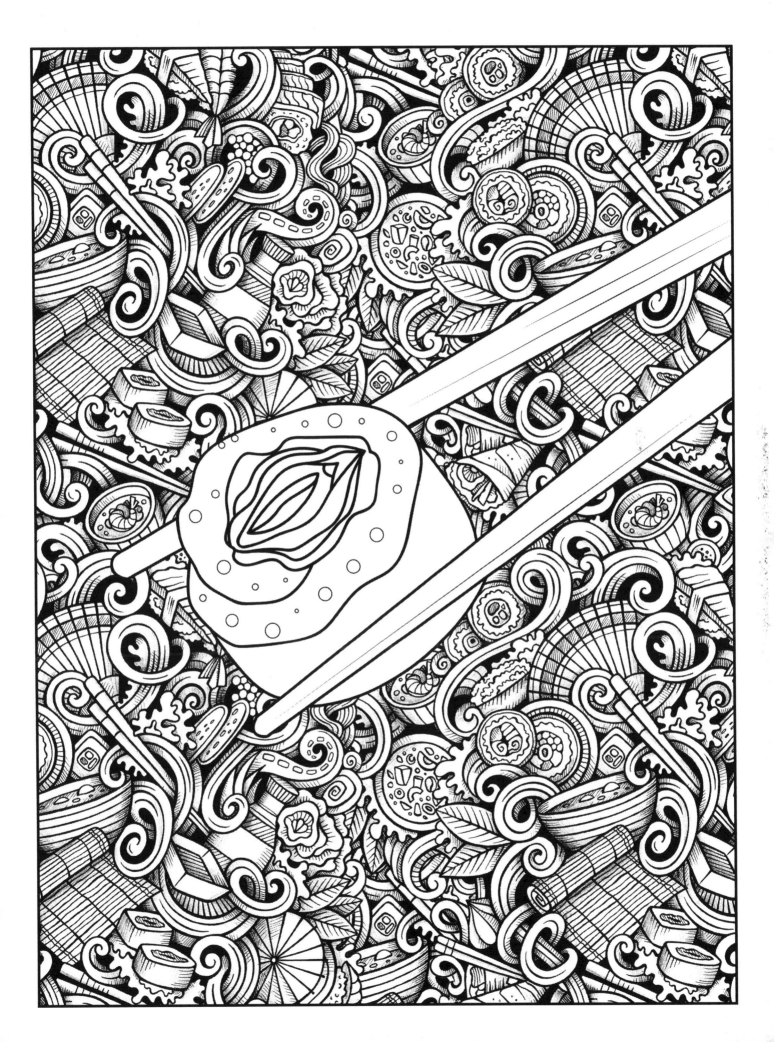

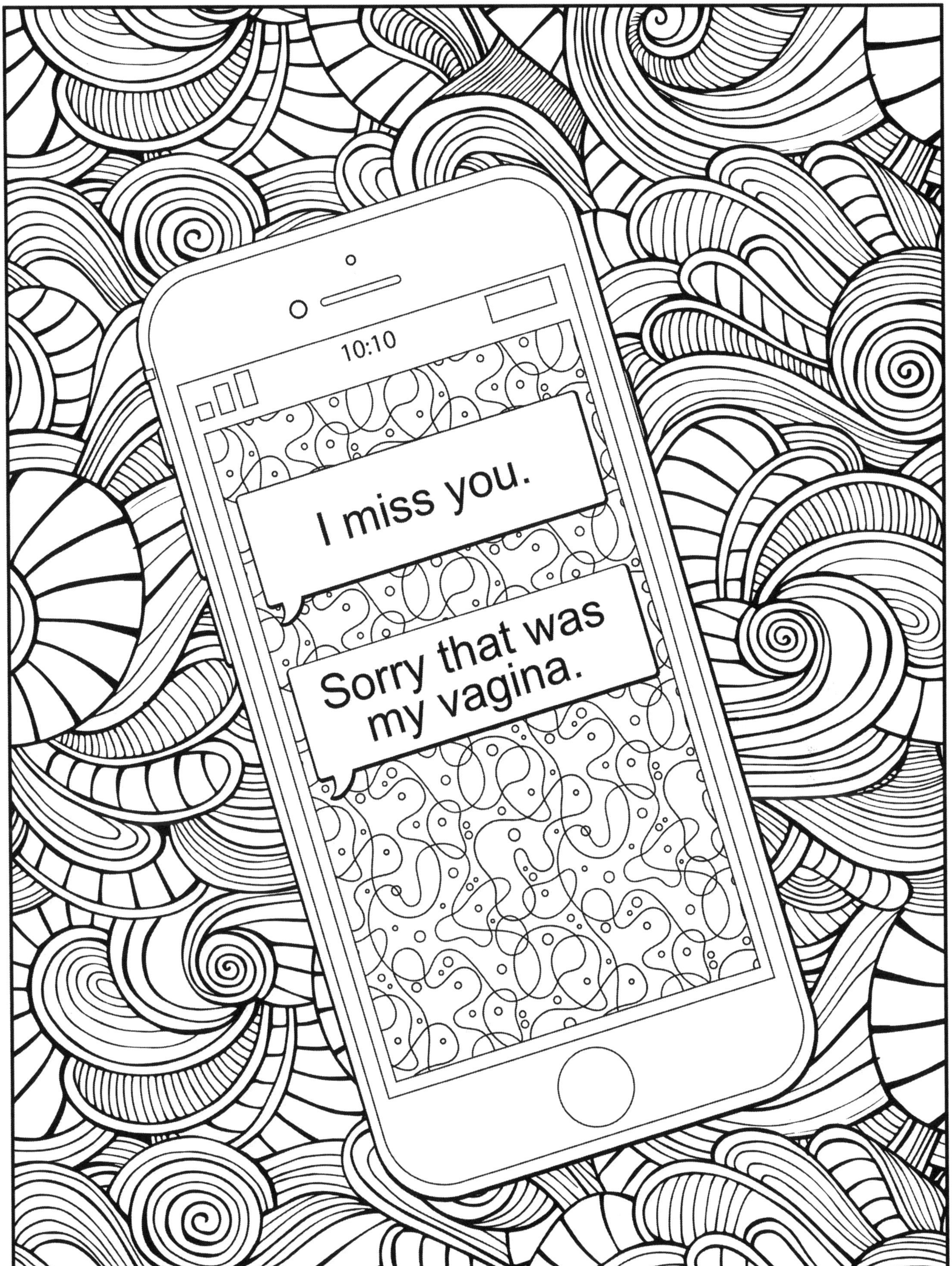
10:10
I miss you.
Sorry that was my vagina.

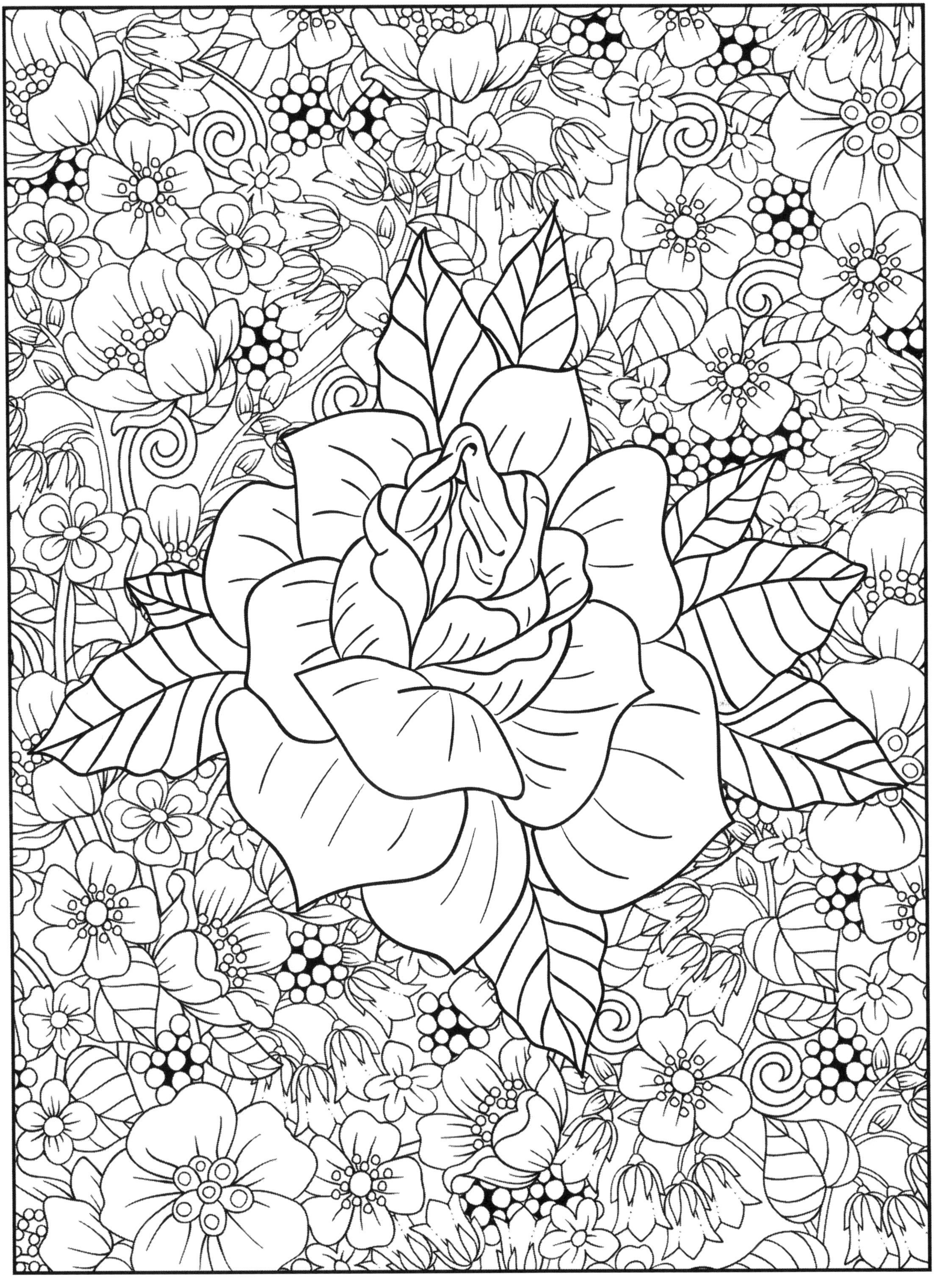

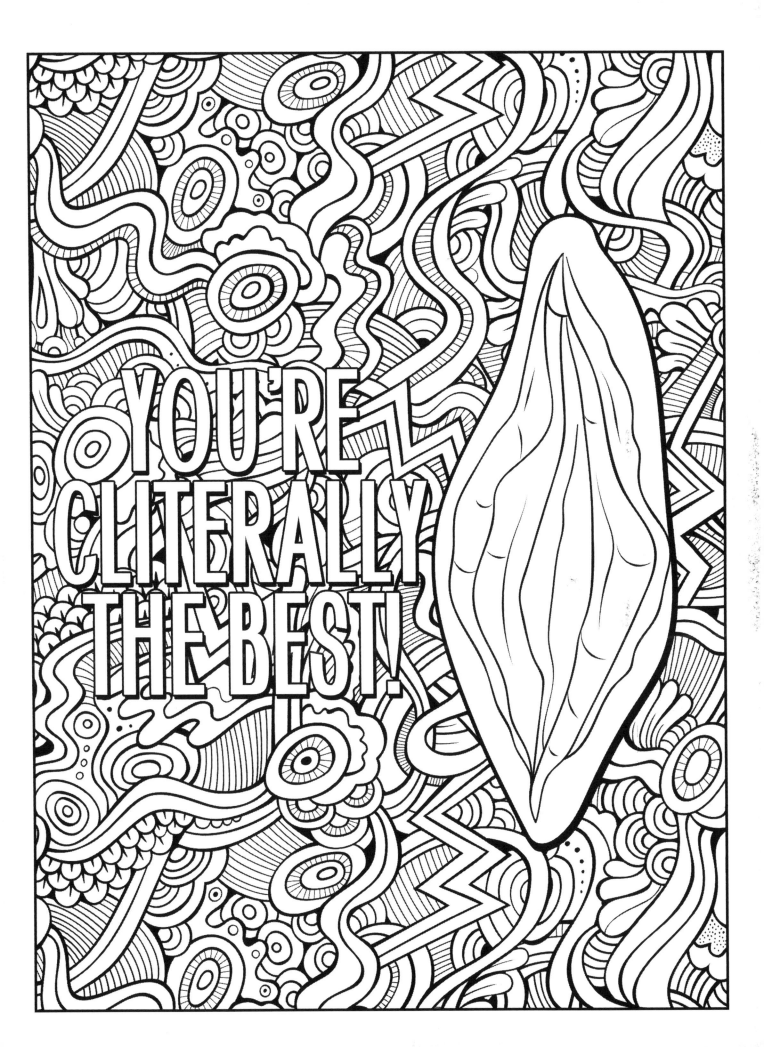

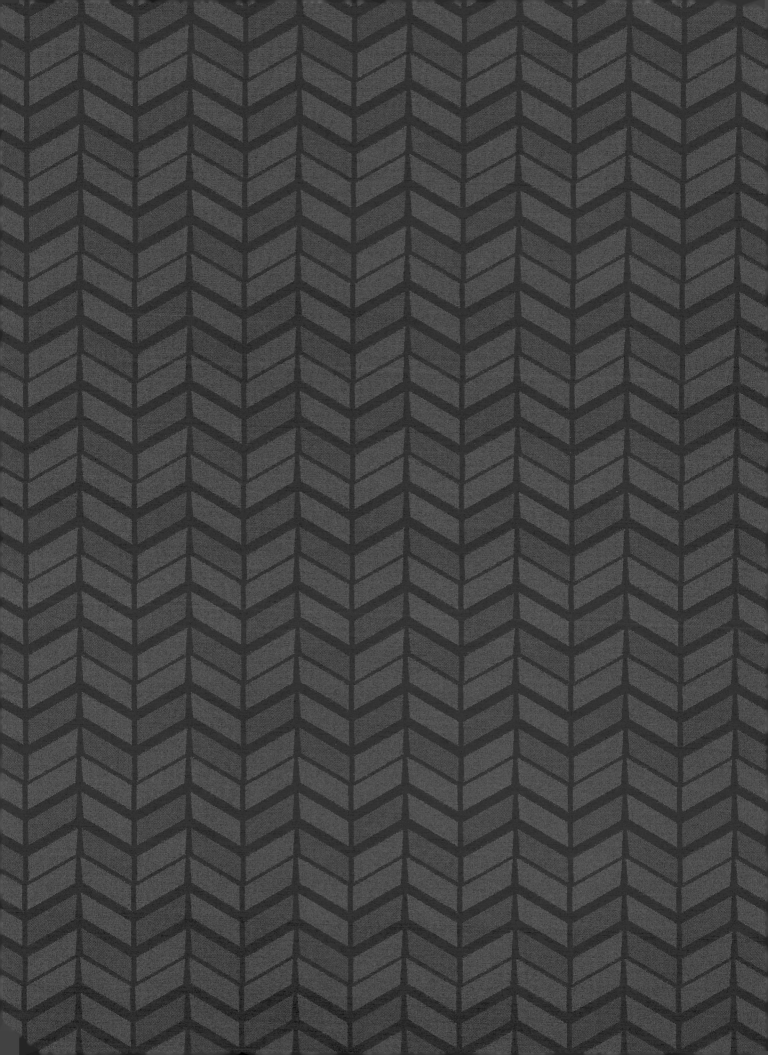

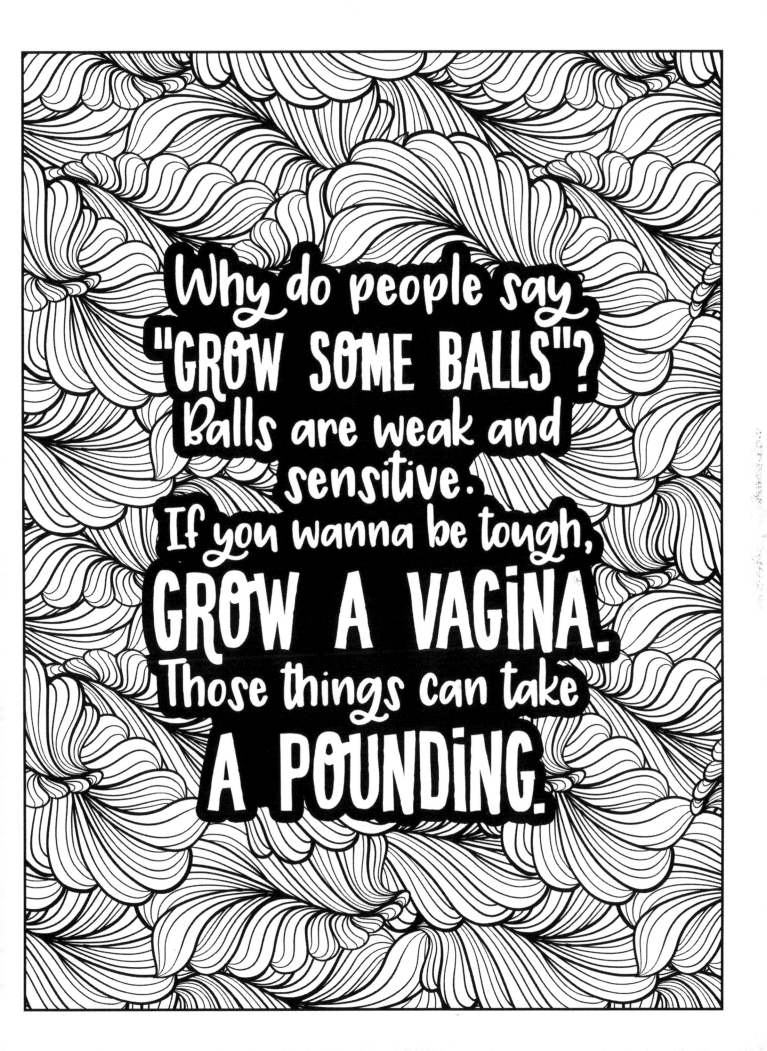

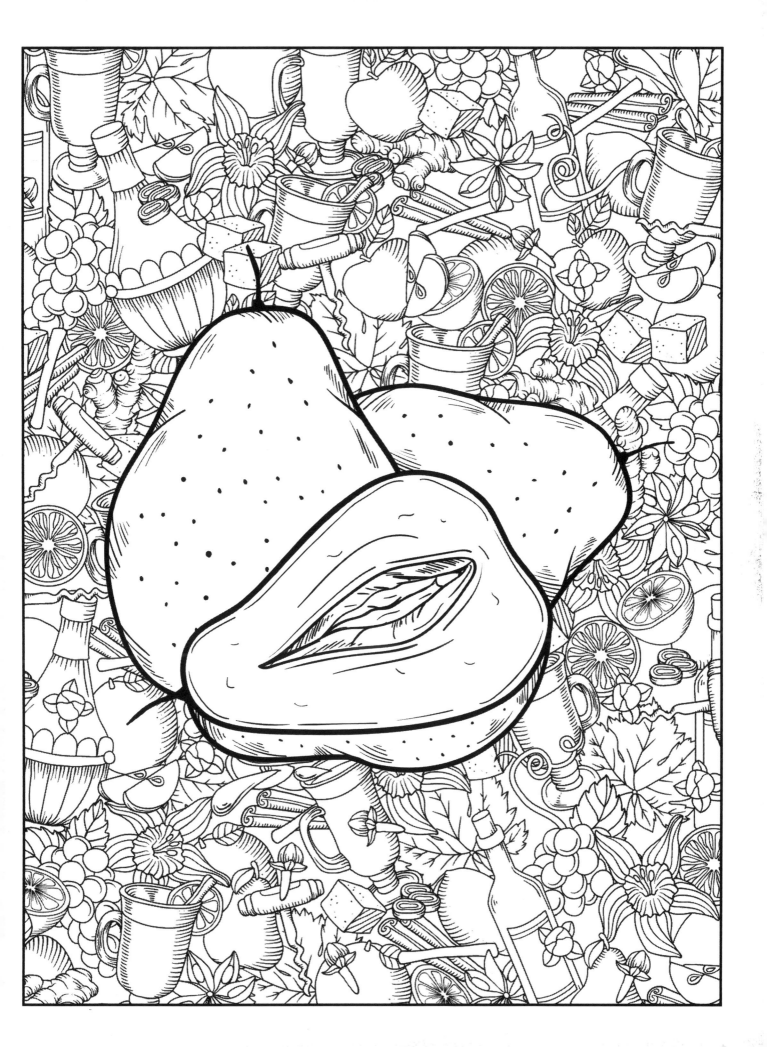

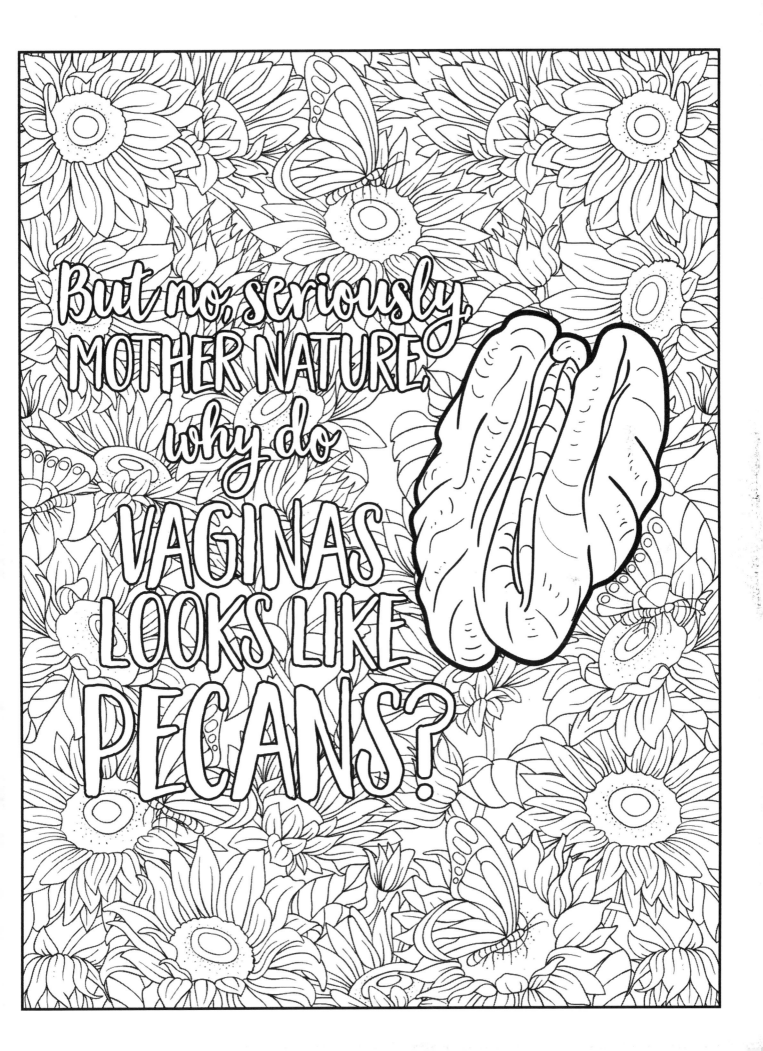

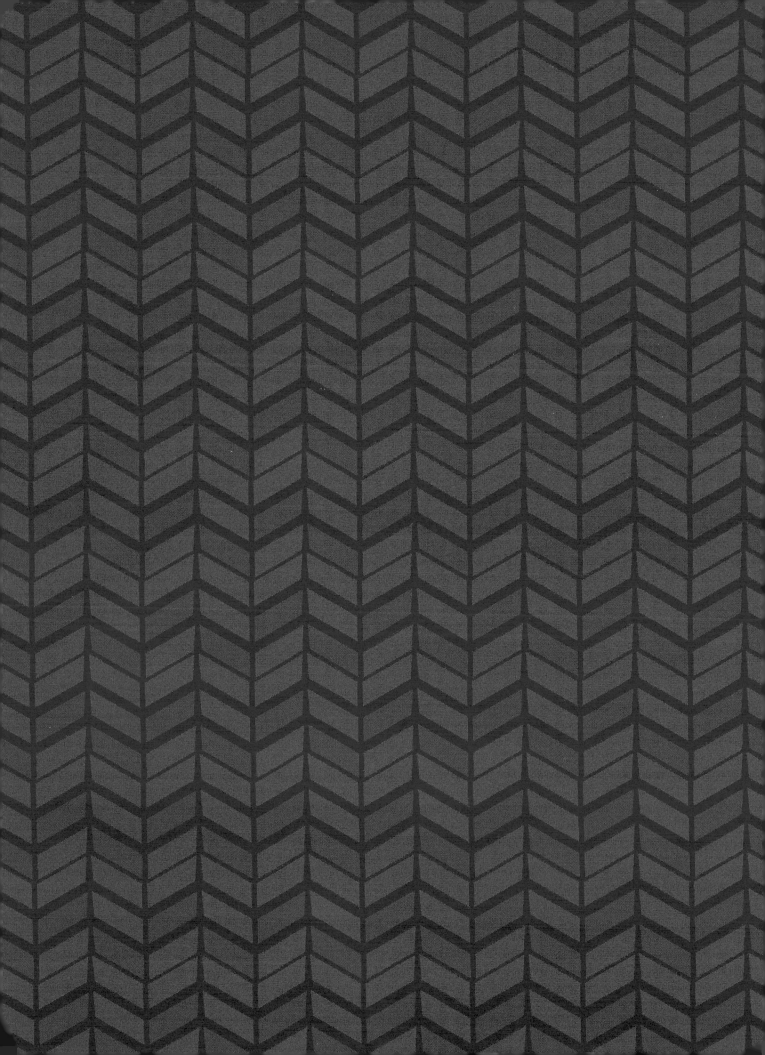

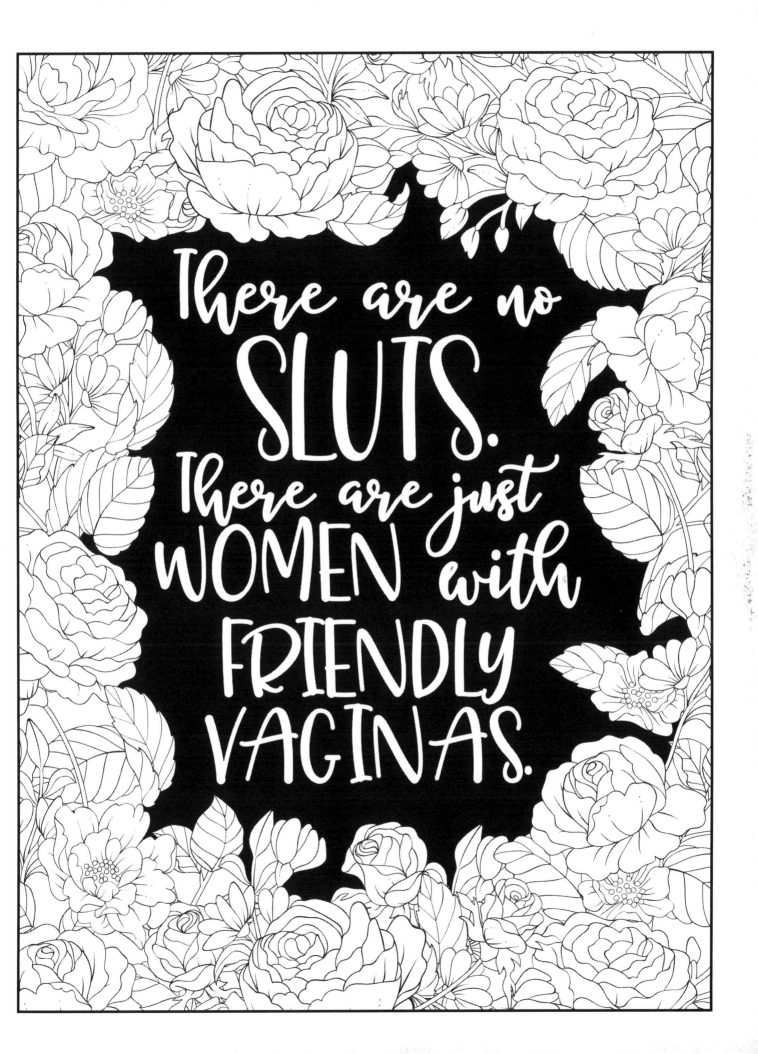

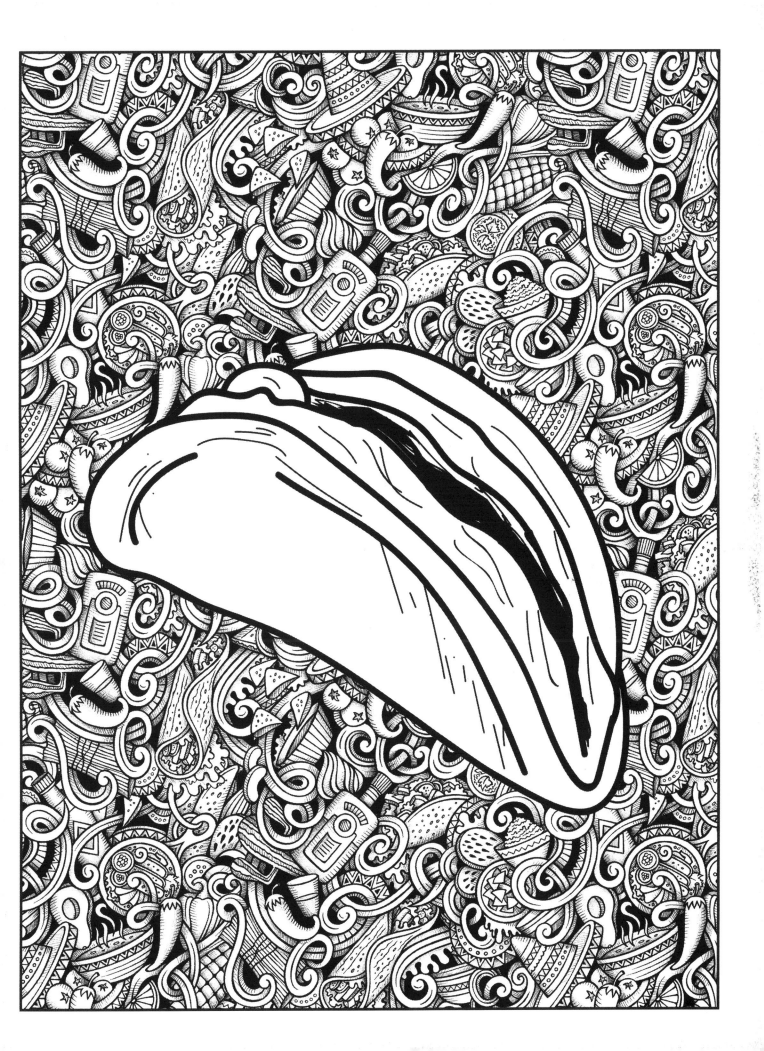

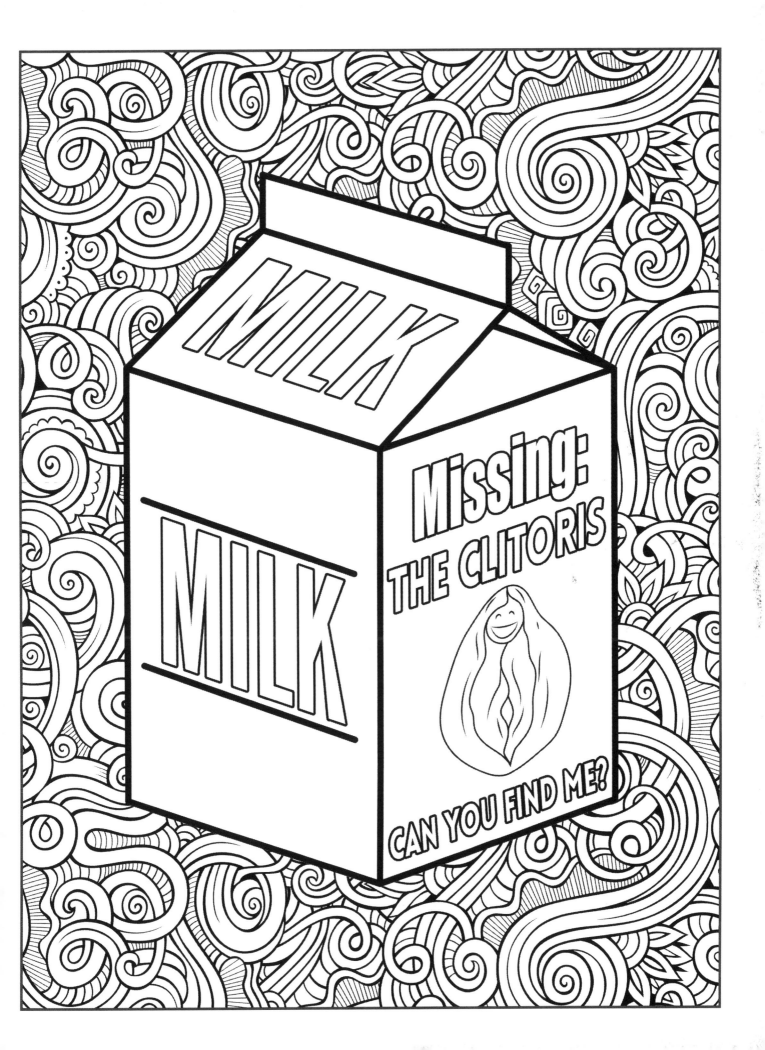

FREE DOWNLOAD!

YOUR CODE: VAG363

www.honeybadgercoloring.com/vajayjay

BE SURE TO FOLLOW US
ON SOCIAL MEDIA FOR THE
LATEST GIVEAWAYS & DISCOUNTS

@honeybadgercoloring

Honey Badger Coloring

@badgercoloring

ADD YOURSELF TO OUR MONTHLY
NEWSLETTER FOR FREE DIGITAL
DOWNLOADS AND DISCOUNT CODES

www.honeybadgercoloring.com/newsletter

CHECK OUT OUR OTHER BOOKS!

www.honeybadgercoloring.com

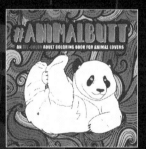

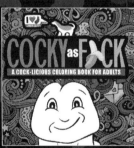

CHECK OUT OUR OTHER BOOKS!

www.honeybadgercoloring.com

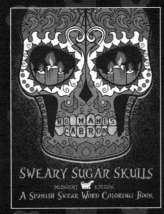
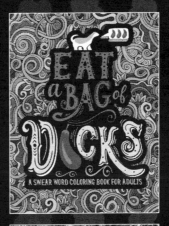

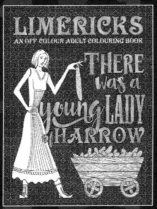

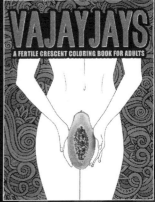

CHECK OUT OUR OTHER BOOKS!

www.honeybadgercoloring.com

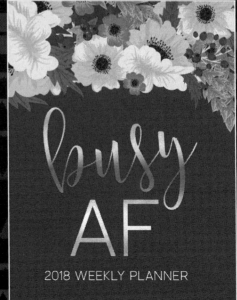

81761540R00046

Made in the USA
Middletown, DE
27 July 2018